T0297482

Messages in the Clouds

Marian S. Taylor

Illustrated by Amy Duarte

Balboa Press books may be ordered through booksellers or by contacting:

Balboa Press
A Division of Hay House
1663 Liberty Drive
Bloomington, IN 47403
www.balboapress.com
844-682-1282

Because of the dynamic nature of the Internet, any web addresses or links contained in this book may have changed since publication and may no longer be valid. The views expressed in this work are solely those of the author and do not necessarily reflect the views of the publisher, and the publisher hereby disclaims any responsibility for them.

Any people depicted in stock imagery provided by Getty Images are models, and such images are being used for illustrative purposes only.
Certain stock imagery © Getty Images.

ISBN: 978-1-5043-7420-0 (sc)
ISBN: 978-1-5043-7421-7 (e)

Library of Congress Control Number: 2017901645

Print information available on the last page.

Balboa Press rev. date: 06/01/2021

Dedication

This book series is dedicated to my husband, our children and grandchildren.

As a little child I come to earth
to experience this wonderful place.

I am excited to be here as I grow and learn
and try to keep up with this dizzying pace.

I want to ask...
Have you ever spent time lying down in the grass...
Looking up at the sky and the clouds floating by?

Have you ever looked up at the sky while in prayer...

And wondered what message might wait for you there?

Have you ever seen an airplane floating by in the sky?

Where is it going and how does it fly?

Have you ever seen an elephant wave its trunk in the wind...

Just tell me what kind of message you think he would send.

Have you ever seen a giant bird flying by?

Or witnessed the appearance of a phoenix on the rise?

Have you ever seen a funny bear resting above the trees?

Or a dragon with outstretched wings gliding on the breeze?

Clouds tell us of storms, of beauty, and of love...

As we marvel at the forms and shapes up above.

For a cloud can tell a story of wind, snow, or rain...

But we always know the sun will come out again.

We know clouds can remind us to feel God's presence...

And experience a bit of heaven's sweet essence.

Take time to relax... to sit and to wonder...

Is a cloud really a cloud when it causes us to ponder...

Stop looking down and begin looking at the sky!

There'll always be a cloud that is more than meets the eye.

About the Author

Marian S. Taylor, EdD, is a retired university professor. Her career began at the elementary level where she taught first grade and served as a reading specialist. She was director of the university laboratory school and a chairperson of a university department. She taught undergraduate and graduate classes while at the university and spent many years directing the program for the development of reading specialists.

Marian has been very involved with her family and with church activities. She is the mother of three grown children and is very proud of her grandchildren.

www.marianstaylor.com

About the Illustrator

Amy Duarte began her career as an artist working for Walt Disney Animaton Studios. From there, she leapt into the world of visual effects and graphic arts on more than 30 feature films like *"Pirates of the Caribbean: At World's End*," *"The Amazing Spiderman*," *"Mr. and Mrs. Smith*," etc. She was appointed as a lead artist for several major motion pictures, including *"Fantastic Four*," where she advised and guided a team of artists on creating the special effects of Jessica Alba's character (Sue Storm).

Born in Jakarta, Indonesia, and raised in three different countries, Amy is fluent in six languages and an avid polo player. She was also on the design team that created the top secret commercial for Apple's Watch before the product was lauched. Her portfolio can be viewed at:

www.amyduarte.com

Printed in the United States
by Baker & Taylor Publisher Services